M000203119

From the
Kitchen
Door

From the Kitchen Door

Dean G. Reeves

Hillsboro Press
Franklin, Tennessee

TENNESSEE HERITAGE LIBRARY
Bicentennial Collection

Copyright 1997 by Dean G. Reeves

Printed in the United States of America

01   00   99   98   97   5   4   3   2   1

Library of Congress Catalog Card Number: 97-75783

ISBN: 1-57736-074-5

Cover design by Gary Bozeman

Recipe consultant—Shirley B. Jones

Published by
HILLSBORO PRESS
an imprint of
PROVIDENCE HOUSE PUBLISHERS
238 Seaboard Lane • Franklin, Tennessee 37067
800-321-5692

In loving memory of
my mother

Lyssa Dean Hunt Gillespie

whose recipes delighted
so many
through the years.

Contents

As a young person, Mother was a beautiful ballet dancer. She later went to music school in Chicago, where she became a wonderful pianist and met my father.

Preface

Lyssa Dean Hunt Gillespie was born in Murfreesboro, Tennessee—the daughter of a wonderful cook. She was not a gourmet cook, by today's standards, but a good, basic, old-fashioned southern cook. She didn't use lots of herbs or fancy new products. She would never have a microwave—couldn't even give her one. She liked cooked fresh vegetables and fruits. She used lard, Parkay oleo, extra large eggs—nothing dietetic or light. She felt the Fannie Farmer cookbook was the best.

It was hard to get a recipe from her because a lot of times there were no amounts or cooking times. When I'd ask her, she'd say—"Oh! you know—when it tastes right, or looks right or feels right."

In 1951, she and a very close friend, Mrs. William J. Bryan (Clara), started doing a little catering out of our house but Clara didn't keep with it too long. Mother's catering business grew and grew. She was one of the first to fix a picnic lunch or supper. They were either in a white box or basket. There was a fried chicken breast (a leg was added if it was for supper), a deviled egg, a piece of garlic pickle, always a tomato sandwich, and either a cream cheese and olive sandwich or a nut bread sandwich, and then a chess pie.

If you ordered food from Mother, she would have you bring your own casserole dish or cake tray so the food would have more of a personal touch when served in your home. She never delivered. For those who came to pick up their food, she hung a sign on the front door knob so folks would know to come around to the kitchen entrance.

PLEASE COME
TO SIDE DOOR

Mother, with the help of Luvada Maney and Goldie Armstrong, who had been with her for years, stayed very active and cooked until her death in 1990. Friends and family still ask for "Mrs. Gillespie's" recipes and reminisce about her delicious, beautifully decorated cakes that were guaranteed to make any occasion a special one.

1

Appetizers and Sandwiches

CHEDDAR BALLS

1/2 pound sharp cheddar cheese, finely grated
1/4 pound butter
1 1/8 cups flour
1/2 teaspoon baking powder
    dash of salt
1 teaspoon of Worcestershire sauce or to taste

Allow grated cheese and butter to reach soft room temperature. Mix all ingredients well.

Cover dough with a damp cloth or paper towel and chill in refrigerator for 1 hour. Shape firm dough into small (about 1 inch) balls. Place on baking sheet 1 1/2 inches apart. Bake at 450 degrees about 7 minutes. Do not brown. Cool before removing from baking sheet.

CHEESE-SAUSAGE BALLS

4 cups Bisquick
1 pound hot sausage
1 10-ounce package Cracker Barrel sharp cheddar cheese,
   finely grated

Allow grated cheese and sausage to reach soft room temperature. Mix all ingredients well. Chill dough well for 1 to 2 hours in the refrigerator. Shape firm dough into 1 1/2 inch balls. Place 2 inches apart on baking sheet. Bake at 400 degrees about 20 minutes.

Note: Dough is easier to handle and will not stick to your hands if you moisten them with cooking oil.

CHEESE STRAWS

1 stick butter or oleo
1/2 pound sharp cheddar cheese, finely grated
2 cups flour
   dash of salt
   Worcestershire sauce to taste
   Tabasco sauce to taste

Allow grated cheese and butter to reach soft room temperature. Mix well with all purpose flour, salt, approximately 1 teaspoon Worcestershire sauce and 1 or 2 hard dashes of hot pepper (Tabasco) sauce. Fill a cookie press with the soft dough and press in long strips onto a baking sheet. Using table knife, cut pressed dough into 2- or 3-inch lengths. Bake at 425 degrees about 8 minutes. Do not brown. Cool before removing from baking sheet. These freeze really well.

ICEBOX CHEESE WAFERS

This recipe was from Lyssa's mother, Willie Haynes Hunt, so note the term "icebox."

1/2 pound cheddar cheese, finely grated
1/4 pound butter
1 1/2 cups flour
    dash of salt
    dash of pepper

Allow grated cheese and butter to reach soft room temperature and cream together. Slowly add flour, salt, and ground pepper. When mixed well, using hands make a roll of the dough 1 1/2 to 2 inches in diameter. Wrap the roll in a damp cloth [foil] and chill overnight in the icebox [refrigerator]. Dough must be chilled and hard in order to slice thinly with a sharp knife. Place wafers on baking sheet. Bake in preheated oven at 425 degrees for 10 to 14 minutes. Do not brown. Cool on a rack after removing from baking sheet.

Note: Rewrap dough and replace in refrigerator if all the wafers cannot be baked at one time. Slice only when ready to bake.

SAUSAGE ROLL

This is a decorative appetizer as the finished wafer resembles a pinwheel.

Make pastry recipe on p. 65. Roll pastry thin. Remove 1 1/2 pounds pork sausage from package and let warm to room temperature. Using spatula or hands spread the softened (still raw) sausage evenly over pastry, leaving 1/4 inch of bare pastry on all edges. Moisten pastry edges with water. Make into a roll and refrigerate several hours or overnight. Dough must be very hard in order to slice into thin wafers, about 1/4 inch. Place slices on baking sheet—not touching. Bake at 400 degrees for about 15 minutes. Do not brown. Cool before removing from baking sheet.

HOT CHEESE DIP

Serve heated in chafing dish with Fritos.

   1   small clove garlic, mashed
   1   10 3/4 ounce can Campbell's cream of mushroom soup
   1   6 ounce roll garlic cheese
1/2   pound Velveeta cheese
   1   beef bouillon cube dissolved in 1/4 cup hot water
       dash Tabasco sauce
   1   tablespoon Worcestershire sauce

Put cream of mushroom soup (undiluted) in top of double boiler. Dissolve the beef bouillon cube in hot water and add to soup. Add mashed up garlic, Worcestershire sauce and Tabasco sauce, stirring well and frequently. When steaming, add garlic cheese and Velveeta cheese in small chunks and heat, stirring until cheese is melted and completely blended with other ingredients.

CLAM DIP

   2   10 ounce cans minced clams, drained
   1   8 ounce package Philadelphia cream cheese
   3   tablespoons lemon juice
   2   tablespoons Worcestershire sauce
   2   tablespoons minced onion
   2   tablespoons ketchup
   1   tablespoon prepared horseradish
   1   teaspoon salt
       dash red pepper

Soften package of cream cheese to room temperature and then add rest of ingredients. Using a mixer, blend all ingredients thoroughly. Chill dip for several hours or overnight. Serve chilled.

RUM DIP FOR RAW VEGETABLES

1 cup homemade mayonnaise (see recipe on p. 24)
1 tablespoon light rum
1 teaspoon garlic salt
1 teaspoon green pepper, finely chopped
1 teaspoon chili sauce

Mix well and chill.

Mother at work in the kitchen.

DEVILED EGGS

Deviled eggs are a year 'round southern favorite and served on all occasions.

6 eggs, hard-boiled
mayonnaise
salt
celery seed
vinegar
juice from garlic pickles (see recipe below)

Slice hard-boiled eggs in half lengthwise. Gently remove yolks from the whites, reserving whites. Mash egg yolks with enough mayonnaise to make a very stiff paste. Add salt and celery seed to taste. Add vinegar and juice from garlic pickles. Use a ratio of 1/4 teaspoon of vinegar to 3/4 teaspoon pickle juice. Mix in well after each addition and taste. Continue this process until you reach desired taste. Spoon yolk mixture into egg white shells. Chill before serving. Sprinkle paprika and parsley on top if halves are served open. If halves are going into a picnic supper, press 2 halves together and wrap in waxed paper. Makes 12 deviled eggs.

GARLIC PICKLES

This was my Grandmother Hunt's recipe and she always insisted that McCormick's pickling spice made the difference.

2 gallon jars sour pickles
10 pounds of sugar
1 jar McCormick's mixed pickling spices
1 pint white vinegar
1 button of garlic, chopped

Drain pickles. Slice and put in large bowl. Cover with ice for several hours. Drain. Add sugar, spices, and vinegar. After the first day, add garlic. Let stand for 5 days. Stir several times making sure the syrup is clear. Put pickles in jars.

TOMATO SANDWICHES

Mother always used Sunbeam thin sliced white bread for her party sandwiches. Sometimes she did use whole wheat bread. She kept bread in the freezer so it would be easier to cut off the crusts or to cut into rounds for tomato sandwiches.

She was really noted for her tomato sandwiches. People would go to parties and be so thrilled when they saw Mrs. Gillespie's tomato sandwiches. But you must use homemade mayonnaise (see recipe on p. 24), onion, peeled tomatoes, and no salt. Use thin sliced white bread since other types of bread would overpower the delicate taste of the mayonnaise and tomato.

Prepare bread rounds. The bread cuts better and will not mash down if frozen. Use a round cutter the size of a tomato slice. Spread with mayonnaise, to which a little grated onion has been added.

To each 1/2 cup of homemade mayonnaise add 1/2 teaspoon fresh finely grated onion with juice.

Use firm, fully ripe tomatoes, peeled. (To make peeling easier, drop the tomato into rapidly boiling water for 30 seconds. This works best on homegrown tomatoes.)

EGG SALAD SANDWICHES

Allow 1 1/2 eggs per generous sandwich. Finely chop hard-boiled eggs. Add 1 teaspoon of mayonnaise, a dash of salt, and 1/8 teaspoon of dried dill weed per 2 eggs. With a fork, mix to a thick, spreadable consistency. Adjust mayonnaise up or down as desired. Chill well before spreading on bread.

2

Salads and Salad Dressings

AVOCADO HALVES WITH HOT SAUCE

Wonderful first course!

6 avocados, ripe, unpeeled, halved, and pitted	3 tablespoons Worcestershire sauce
1 cup ketchup	1 tablespoon vinegar
1 1/2 cup water	2–3 teaspoons horseradish
2 tablespoons butter	1/2 mashed button of garlic
2 tablespoons sugar	salt and pepper to taste

Heat all sauce ingredients until thick. Slice each avocado in half and remove seed. Spoon hot sauce into the hollow seed pit of the avocado halves and serve. Sauce keeps well and may be made ahead.

18

CONGEALED AVOCADO

 2 packages gelatin
 1 cup cold water
1/2 cup lemon juice
 4 tablespoons sugar
 1 teaspoon salt
 2 avocados, mashed
 1 cup mayonnaise
 1 cup unsweetened whipped cream

Sprinkle gelatin into cold water. Heat, stirring constantly to dissolve gelatin. Remove from heat and stir in sugar to dissolve. Cool gelatin. Add salt and lemon juice to mashed avocados and add all to cooled gelatin. Chill mixture in refrigerator until it begins to thicken. Add mayonnaise and unsweetened whipped cream. Blend thoroughly with a fork or wire whisk. Turn mixture into an oiled mold and chill until set. Serves 8.

Note: Unflavored gelatin is usually packaged in 1/4 ounce envelopes, 4 envelopes per box.

CHERRY SALAD

 1 cup pitted canned black bing cherries
 1 cup canned pineapple, drained
 1 envelope gelatin
1/2 cup cold water
 1 lemon, juiced
1 1/2 cups fruit juice

Drain canned fruits, reserving juices. Soak gelatin in cold water for five minutes as directed. Heat in the top of a double boiler stirring constantly until gelatin is dissolved. Remove from heat and add to lemon juice and 1 1/2 cups of reserved fruit juices mixed. Chill mixture in refrigerator until it begins to thicken. Add mixed fruits and stir to mix evenly. Turn mixture into an oiled mold and chill until set.

CRANBERRY SALAD

2 cups raw cranberries
1 orange, cut in segments
1 whole apple, chopped
1/2 cup celery, chopped
1 package lemon or orange gelatin
1 cup sugar
1 cup boiling water
1/2 cup cold water
   dash of salt

Put the cranberries and orange segments through a food chopper. Mix with the apple and celery. Dissolve together the gelatin, sugar, and boiling water. Add the cold water and salt to gelatin. Let gelatin set until it is partially congealed, then stir in the fruit mixture and turn into molds as desired.

The sugar may be added to cranberries and orange peel instead of being dissolved in the hot water if there's time for it to stand a few minutes before being combined.

MELON BALLS WITH SAUCE

This recipe came from Attie Chalfant, a good friend and neighbor for many years.

1/2 cup sugar
1/3 cup water
  2 tablespoons lemon juice
  2 tablespoons lime juice
  2 tablespoons orange juice

Cook sugar and water for 5 minutes. Cool. Add lemon juice, lime juice, and orange juice. Pour over assorted melon balls.

SLAW

  1 small head cabbage, grated
  1 small red bell pepper, finely chopped
  1 small green bell pepper, finely chopped
  1 large onion, finely chopped
  1 small bunch celery, finely chopped
  1 teaspoon mustard seed
  1 teaspoon celery seed
  1 cup sugar
1/2 teaspoon salt
1/4 teaspoon pepper
  1 cup vinegar
  1 cup water

Add finely chopped peppers, onion, and celery to grated cabbage. Add remaining dry ingredients and mix well in a large bowl. Add cold water and vinegar and mix very well. Cover bowl and chill, stirring occasionally until time to serve.

CONGEALED SLAW

1 small green cabbage, finely grated	1 cup celery, finely chopped
	2 envelopes Knox gelatin
1/2 cup green pepper, finely grated	2 cups cold water
	3/4 cup vinegar
1/2 cup red bell pepper, finely chopped	3/4 cup sugar
	1/2 teaspoon salt

Mix together well the finely grated or shredded cabbage, green pepper, red bell pepper, and celery.

Sprinkle the Knox gelatin into cold water. Heat, stirring constantly to dissolve gelatin. Remove from heat and add sugar. Stir to dissolve. Add vinegar and salt. Chill until mixture begins to thicken. Add vegetable mixture and stir well to mix. Place in oiled mold and chill to set.

HATTIE POST'S CONGEALED SALAD

Hattie Post was a friend of Mother's from Murfreesboro and lived across the street on Deer Park Circle. Note on "India" relish: This is Indian relish which is a chopped green tomato relish or chow-chow. It is sometime called green tomato chutney.

      2   3 ounce packages lemon Jello
      1   cup pecans, chopped
      4   tablespoons "India" relish
      1   cup pimento-stuffed olives, chopped
      1   cup celery, chopped
   1/4   cup green pepper, chopped

Make lemon Jello according to package directions, leaving out 1/2 cup of water. Allow Jello to cool until it begins to thicken. Add coarsely chopped pecans and coarsely chopped pimento-stuffed green olives. Add celery and green pepper, chopped to a medium small consistency, and 4 table-spoons Indian relish. Pour into an oiled 2 quart mold and refrigerate until set. Makes 7 1/2 cups or 15 half-cup servings. For a garnish use artichokes and cream cheese balls.

CHICKEN SALAD

Cover chicken breast halves in water and a little salt. Cook for 45 minutes to an hour until tender.

Remove skin and bone from cooked chicken and discard. Coarsely chop chicken. Mix with 1/2 cup finely chopped celery. Add homemade mayonnaise (see recipe on p. 24), salt, and freshly grated onion to taste. Should not be soupy. Chill.

POTATO SALAD

The amount of potato salad you make depends on the number of servings you need. Allow 1/2 cup of salad per serving.

Choose four unpeeled white baking potatoes of a uniform size and shape. Wash, place in a boiler, and add cold water to completely cover. Heat to boiling, reduce heat, cover, and boil until tender. Do not overcook. After 15 minutes of boiling, test by piercing one potato with a fork. If the fork goes into potato without being forced, potato is done. If not, continue to boil, checking for doneness every 5 minutes. Do not overcook or the potatoes will start to fall apart.

Completely cool the potatoes. Skin them and dice into cubes approximately one inch square. (Uniformity of cubes is not important.) For 4 cups of potato cubes add 2/3 cup of finely sliced or chopped celery, 1/3 cup finely chopped green pepper, 3 ounce jar of chopped pimento, drained, and 1 teaspoon celery seed. Add homemade mayonnaise (see recipe on p. 24) to desired consistency. Stir. Add freshly grated onion with juice and salt to taste. Chill for several hours or overnight to allow the flavors to blend and strengthen before serving.

CELERY SEED SALAD DRESSING

1 1/2 cups Crisco oil	1/2 tablespoon celery seed
3/4 cup sugar	1/2 tablespoon paprika
1/2 cup vinegar	1/2 tablespoon salt
1/2 cup ketchup	1/2 tablespoon grated onion

Mix all ingredients well. Chill before serving. Store in refrigerator. Makes 1 quart plus 1 1/4 cups.

MAYONNAISE

Homemade mayonnaise is the secret to so many of Mother's recipes: chicken salad, tomato sandwiches, etc.

5 egg yolks, extra large	dash red pepper
2 teaspoons sugar	1 quart regular Wesson oil
2 teaspoons salt	2 teaspoons white vinegar
1 teaspoon dry mustard	juice of 2 lemons
dash paprika	

In a mixer, beat egg yolks then add next 5 ingredients. **Slowly** start adding oil. When half of oil is used, add white vinegar and lemon juice. You can use frozen lemon juice. Add remaining oil. Lastly add about 3 to 4 tablespoons boiling water to make it smoother.

Notes: If not using extra large eggs for this mayonnaise, use 1/2 cup of egg yolks. Use a high speed in mixing. The oil (4 cups or 1 quart) must be added very slowly.

3

Main Dishes

FRIED CHICKEN

1 cut-up frying chicken	1 teaspoon paprika
1 cup flour	lard
1/2 teaspoon salt	

Wash chicken pieces very well under cold running water and pat dry. Lightly salt pieces. Place flour, salt, and paprika in paper sack or a plastic bag. Add 1 or 2 pieces of chicken at a time and shake to completely coat with flour mixture, adding more flour and spices as needed.

Meanwhile preheat a heavy skillet (10 or 12 inches) with 1 inch of melted lard over medium high heat. Discard leftover flour mixture. Place chicken pieces in hot oil and fry to brown, turning chicken pieces as needed. When all the chicken pieces are a golden brown, reduce to low heat, tightly cover, and cook very slowly until fork tender. Drain well.

WELSH RAREBIT

This makes a good Sunday night supper.

> 1 tablespoon butter
> 2 tablespoons flour or 1 teaspoon cornstarch
> 1/2 cup milk
> 1/4 teaspoon salt
> 1/2 pound sharp cheddar cheese, grated
> 1/4 teaspoon dry mustard
>   dash red pepper
>   dash Worcestershire sauce
>   dash Tabasco sauce

In the top of a double boiler, over medium heat melt butter and add flour, stirring constantly. Allow to cook 1 minute. Still stirring constantly, slowly add milk. Now add the grated cheese a handful at a time. Continue stirring until cheese is all melted and smooth. Stir in dry mustard and a dash each of red (cayenne) pepper, Worcestershire sauce, and Tabasco sauce.

When sauce is smooth and spoonable, serve over toast rounds or triangles. If not smooth, using electric mixer beat 1 whole egg until a uniform lemony color. While still beating add 1 cup of the cheese sauce 1 tablespoon at a time. Then transfer this mixture back to the double boiler, stirring into balance of sauce. This should remove the stringiness.

CHICKEN RAGOUT

6–7 pounds chicken, cooked and chopped	2 teaspoons salt
1 small whole onion	1 28 ounce can tomatoes
1 rib celery	1/2 pound or less of rice
1 large onion, chopped	1 cup slivered almonds
1 green pepper, chopped	1 cup white raisins
	1 teaspoon pepper

Place raw chicken breasts (or breasts and thighs) in a very large pot. Add salt, pepper, whole onion, and celery. Cover with cold water, bring to a boil. Cover pot and simmer for 45 minutes or until chicken is tender. Remove chicken and cool. Discard onion and celery rib and reserve stock. Remove and discard skin and bones from chicken. Then coarsley chop chicken.

In the bottom of a large (at least 6 quart) pot, heat 1 tablespoon oil over medium heat. Add coarsely chopped onion and coarsely chopped green pepper. Cook, stirring until onion is transparent. Add chicken and can of tomatoes. Simmer until thick. Add 1 1/2 cups uncooked, white long-grained rice (not instant or quick cooking). Thin with 2 1/2 cups of reserved chicken stock. Add blanched slivered almonds and raisins. Return pan to heat, bring to a boil, reduce heat, and simmer 20 minutes until rice is tender. May need to add small amounts of chicken stock or water if the mixture begins to stick or get too dry. Serve hot. Serves 12.

TENNESSEE COUNTRY HAM

Mother bought her hams from a man in Columbia who aged and cured them. H. G. Hill's hams are good.

This is a dangerous recipe! "Country Ham" is the type or kind of ham—not the name of the recipe. At the time Lyssa first developed her recipe, country ham was the norm. Now it is an expensive, gourmet item. The usual baked ham, honey glazed ham or spiral sliced ham is a "water added" ham. Country ham is a "water depleted" ham, from a curing process that takes from 4 to 12 months. The longer the curing process the drier and more expensive the ham. Country hams cost at least 3 to 5 times more than "city ham." They are usually sold in a cotton drawstring sack.

This recipe must be started at least 24 to 36 hours before serving. Unless you have more than 1 oven, you should consider doing the initial 10 hour baking overnight. As long as the ham is completely sealed in foil, undercooking is more of a problem than a little overcooking.

Cut off hock (or have the store you buy from cut off the hock for you). Reserve hock.

Wash the ham well under lukewarm running water. Scrub it completely with a stiff brush. Completely cover the ham with cold water and soak it for at least 10 to 12 hours. If time constraints force you to soak the ham 2 or 3 hours more, drain off the old water and add fresh cold water for the additional soaking time.

Drain the water from the ham. Place the ham in the bottom of a roasting pan. Slice 2 unpeeled tart apples and place the slices on top of the ham.

Seal the ham completely with heavy duty foil even if your roast pan has a tight fitting lid. Bake at 250 degrees for approximately 10 hours. The meat must reach 160 degrees on a meat thermometer. Remove the ham from roasting pan. Remove the skin. Trim the fat until it is no more than 1/2 inch thick and not less than 1/4 inch thin. Score fat in a criss-cross pattern.

Make a thick paste using 1 cup brown sugar, 1/2 teaspoon ground cinnamon, and enough apple cider vinegar to moisten. Spread the paste onto all the upper surfaces of the ham and spear about one handful of whole cloves over the surface in a random pattern. Bake 45 minutes in a preheated 350 degree oven. Remove from oven and let stand about 20 minutes prior to slicing and serving.

BARBEQUE SAUCE

This is a good barbeque sauce for chicken, pork—whatever!

1 cup water	1/4 cup ketchup
1/4 cup sugar	1 teaspoon salt
1/2 cup vinegar	1/2 teaspoon pepper
1/4 cup minced onion	1 teaspoon paprika
1/4 pound butter	1 1/2 tablespoons Worcestershire
1 tablespoon flour	sauce

Combine all ingredients in a nonaluminum sauce pan over medium heat. Bring to a boil. Reduce heat and simmer for 15 minutes. Stir frequently. Makes approximately 16 ounces. Store refrigerated until ready to use.

BAKED LARGE WHOLE SALMON

1 8 to 10 pound whole salmon
1 pound salt-free butter

Wash fish well, grease inside and out with cooking oil, sprinkle with salt and place in a glass baking dish. Begin baking salmon in an oven preheated to 550 degrees. After 10 to 15 minutes reduce temperature to 425 degrees and continue cooking for an additional 30 minutes to an hour. (A 10-pounder requires an hour for final cooking period.)

Remove fish from oven and cool in the dish in which it was baked. After it is cool, chill in the refrigerator until it is cold throughout. Beat the butter until creamy. Optional: Tint butter to a nice shade of green and use to frost cold baked salmon as if it were a cake. Place on large wooden tray or board garnished with parsley and lemon slices. Serve with melba toast rounds and a sour cream and dill sauce.

Mother's photo from the Nashville Tennessean, *November 25, 1958.*

4

Casseroles and Side Dishes

CHEESE GRITS

Cheese grits are a family staple and a party favorite to be served at breakfast, luncheon, dinner, brunch, or for an evening buffet supper.

- 1 cup dry grits
- 1 roll garlic cheese
- 1 stick butter
- 2 eggs, beaten

Cook dry grits according to package directions. This yields 3 cups of cooked grits. Grits must be thick enough to be eaten gracefully with a fork. You may use quick (5 minute) grits but **do not use instant** grits.

When grits are cooked, stir in garlic cheese roll cut into chunks and butter cut into chunks. Beat eggs and add to grits. Mix well. Before serving bake in preheated 350 degree oven for 20 minutes to heat through and allow the eggs to "set." Do not brown. Can be made the day before.

31

CHEESE CASSEROLE

12 slices Sunbeam thin sliced bread
1/2 pound sharp cheddar cheese
2 2/3 cups milk
4 extra large eggs
paprika
3/4 teaspoon salt
1/4 teaspoon pepper
Worcestershire sauce to taste
Tabasco sauce, several dashes

Slice cheese into 6 equal slices. Butter a 9 x 13 inch baking dish generously. Trim crusts from bread and lay six slices onto bottom of baking dish. Slice cheese and layer on bread. Place remaining six slices of bread on top. In a large mixing bowl beat eggs (if using Grade A large eggs increase to 5) until smooth and lemony. Add milk, salt, white pepper or finely ground black pepper, 1 or 2 teaspoons Worcestershire sauce, and several (2 to 4) dashes of Tabasco sauce.

Pour mixture over bread and cheese, sprinkle with paprika, and chill overnight. Bake in a preheated 350 degree oven for 1 hour or until mixture is "set" and well browned. Serve hot. Makes 6 entree servings or 12 luncheon servings.

CHICKEN TETRAZZINI

2 cups cooked chicken breast
1/2 pound thin spaghetti
1/2 pound sautéed mushrooms or 8 ounce can
1 tablespoon oil
3 tablespoons butter
2 tablespoons flour
2 cups chicken stock
1/2 cup milk
1 teaspoon salt
parmesan cheese
slivered almonds

Remove skin and bone from cooked chicken breasts and discard. Chop enough chicken for 2 cups. Reserve stock. Cook spaghetti according to package directions.

Prepare the cream sauce. Melt butter over medium low heat. Stir in flour. Allow to cook together one minute. Do not brown. Add milk slowly, stirring constantly. Slowly add chicken stock, stirring constantly. Add salt.

Combine chicken, spaghetti, and mushrooms. Add to cream sauce. Transfer to a 3 quart casserole or to 9 x 13 glass baking dish. Sprinkle parmesan cheese and sliced or slivered raw almonds over the top.

Bake in preheated 375 degree oven for 20 minutes to heat. Freezes well.

HOT CHICKEN SALAD CASSEROLE

2 cups cooked chicken
1 cup celery, chopped
1/2 cup Hellmann's mayonnaise
2 tablespoons onions, finely chopped
1 teaspoon of salt or to taste
1/2 cup sliced almonds
1 10 1/2 ounce can Campbell's cream of chicken soup
1 8 ounce can sliced water chestnuts.
1/2 cup crumbled potato chips

Coarsely chop 2 cups cooked chicken (skin and bones removed). Add chopped celery, Hellmann's mayonnaise (mayonnaise is to be cooked so it does not need the delicate flavor of homemade), onions, salt, almonds, Campbell's cream of chicken soup, undiluted, and sliced water chestnuts, well drained. Mix well. Turn into a lightly greased 2 quart casserole dish. Top with potato chips. Bake at 350 degrees for 25 minutes. Serve hot.

MACARONI RING

1 1/2 cups macaroni,   3 tablespoons butter, melted
       cooked and chopped   1 tablespoon onion, minced
1 cup cheddar cheese, diced   1 cup scalded milk
1 cup bread crumbs   1 egg, well beaten
1 tablespoon parsley, minced   1 teaspoon salt
3 tablespoons pimento   1/8 teaspoon pepper

Combine all ingredients in the order given. Bake in a greased ring mold placed in a pan of hot water for 35 minutes at 375 degrees. Good served with cooked English peas in the center.

SEAFOOD CASSEROLE

1   medium green pepper, chopped
1   medium onion, chopped
1   cup celery, chopped
6 1/2   ounce can crab meat
6 1/2   ounce can shrimp
1/2   teaspoon salt
1/8   teaspoon pepper
1   teaspoon Worcestershire sauce
1 1/4   cups mayonnaise
1/4   stick butter
1/2   cup fine dry bread crumbs

Mix together all ingredients. Put into ceramic baking shells. Sprinkle with buttered bread crumbs and paprika. Bake in preheated 350 degree oven for 30 minutes. Serve hot.

Goldie serving at granddaughter Edie's bridesmaid luncheon at Mother's house.

35

TAMALE PIE

2 pounds ground beef	3 teaspoons chili powder
1 medium onion, chopped	salt and pepper to taste
2–3 8 ounce cans tomato sauce	1 6 ounce can pitted ripe olives

Brown ground beef with chopped onion. Drain to remove excess fat. Add tomato sauce, chili powder, 1 teaspoon salt, and 1 teaspoon pepper. Simmer on very low heat for 30 minutes. Remove from heat. Add well drained, pitted ripe olives.

Butter a 9 x 13 inch glass baking dish. Make a crust on bottom 1/2 inch thick and on sides 1/4 inch thick by patting in cool cornmeal mush (see recipe below). Gently fill with meat mixture. Bake in preheated 350 degree oven for 20 minutes. Garnish as desired. Serve hot.

CORN MEAL MUSH

Corn meal mush is an unassuming southern staple which can be dressed up for breakfast with maple syrup, molasses, or honey with or without milk or cream. Or add butter, salt, and pepper to serve as a vegetable (like grits).

1 cup plain corn meal (not cornmeal *mix*)
1/2 teaspoon salt
1 quart (4 cups) boiling water

If using stone ground or whole grain corn meal, sift to remove bran before measuring 1 cup. Slowly add corn meal to boiling water in 2 quart saucepan, stirring constantly. Cook over high heat for 2 to 3 minutes. Reduce heat to very low and slowly simmer 25 to 30 minutes until very thick, stirring frequently. Mush is done when you can dip it on a dinner fork.

CORN PUDDING

4 ears of corn   1/2 cup sugar
1 cup milk   pinch of salt
3 eggs, beaten   butter about twice the size of an egg

Cut corn about half the grain and scrape cob for the other half. In the winter when corn is not too good, I have used frozen or sometimes even canned corn. Beat eggs and combine all ingredients except butter. Pour into a 5 cup to 1 1/2 quart casserole dish and pat with butter. Bake in a 375 to 400 degree oven for 25 to 35 minutes or until pudding is set.

ASPARAGUS CASSEROLE

2 15 ounce cans extra long asparagus spears, drained
3–4 hard-boiled eggs
1 recipe of cream sauce
1/4 cup slivered or sliced almonds

Cream sauce:
    3 tablespoons butter
    2 tablespoons flour
    1 cup half and half (or whole milk)
    1/4 teaspoon white pepper
    1/2 teaspoon salt

Melt butter in a small skillet over medium heat. Add flour, stirring until smooth. Do not brown. Slowly add half and half or milk, stirring constantly. Cook until thickened, stirring constantly to prevent lumping. Add white pepper and salt. Remove from heat.

In a buttered casserole dish put a layer of asparagus and top with sliced hard-boiled eggs. Pour the cream sauce over this. Top with sliced or slivered almonds. Bake at 350 degrees approximately 15 minutes or until heated through.

GREEN BEAN CASSEROLE

3–4 tablespoons butter
1 8 ounce can sliced
  mushrooms or
1 pound fresh mushrooms
1 medium onion, chopped
1/4 cup flour
2 cups milk
1 cup half and half
3/4 pound (12 ounces) sharp
  cheddar cheese, grated

1/2 teaspoon pepper
2 teaspoons soy sauce
1 teaspoon MSG
1/8 teaspoon Tabasco
3–4 10 ounce packages frozen
  French cut green beans
1 5 ounce can of sliced
  water chestnuts, drained and
  diced
  slivered almonds

Sauté sliced mushrooms in butter. Add chopped onion and cook until transparent. Blend in flour until smooth. Stirring constantly, slowly add milk and half and half. Still stirring constantly, add grated cheese, pepper, MSG, Tabasco, and soy sauce. Stir and cook until cheese is melted and sauce is smooth. Remove from heat. Cook green beans according to package directions and drain. Add green beans and water chestnuts to cheese sauce. Mix well. Pour into buttered 3 quart casserole or 9 x 13 baking dish. Sprinkle the top with almonds. Bake at 375 degrees 30 to 40 minutes. Serves 15.

GLACÉED BEETS

2 cups vinegar
2 cups sugar
2 tablespoons cornstarch

1/2 cup cold water
3 14 1/4 to 16 ounce cans
  small whole beets, drained

Boil vinegar and sugar for 5 minutes. Mix cornstarch in cold water. Add to vinegar and sugar and cook until thickened, about 5 minutes. Cool, add beets. Reheat before serving. Makes approximately 3 pints.

BOSTON BAKED BEANS

4	cups dry Navy beans	1/2	pound fat salt pork
10	cups water	1/4	teaspoon dry mustard (yellow)
1	teaspoon salt	4	tablespoons molasses
1	pinch baking soda	1	teaspoon salt
		1	large onion, cut

Wash Navy beans and soak overnight in water with 1 teaspoon of salt. In the morning add baking soda and bring to a rolling boil. Remove from heat. Cover and let stand while dicing salt pork. Drain the beans and put into 3 quart crockery bean pot. Add the diced salt pork, mustard, molasses (not syrup), 1 teaspoon salt, and coarsely chopped onion. Fill pot with water within 1 inch of the top, cover, and bake 8 hours at 250 degrees. If not sweet enough, add more molasses. Makes about 12 generous servings.

BAKED FRUIT

1	pound can peaches
1	pound can pears
1	pound can apricots
1	pound can cherries
1	pound can crushed pineapple
2	apples or
1	can pie apples, not pie filling
2	bananas
1/2	cup sugar

Drain fruit well. Combine all the juices with sugar. Cook until syrup begins to thicken. Bake fruit in lightly buttered casserole dish at 400 degrees for 40 minutes. Pour fruit juice on syrup and bake at lower temperature for 20 minutes. Can be made ahead and baked the 20 minutes before serving.

CUCUMBER SOUP

I gave this recipe to Mother and she used it a lot. Libby Werthan gave it to me. Wonderful!

2 green onions, chopped
1 small onion, finely chopped
2 tablespoons butter
4 chicken bouillon cubes
3 cups boiling water
1/2 cup parsley, chopped
1/2 cup celery, finely chopped
3 medium potatoes, peeled and quartered
1/2 teaspoon thyme
    dash Tabasco sauce
2 cups sour cream
1 teaspoon salt
1 large cucumber, peeled, seeded, and finely grated

Sauté onions and butter for 5 minutes. Dissolve bouillon in water. Add parsley, onions, celery, and potatoes. Bring to a boil. Cook over low heat 20 minutes. Put cooked ingredients into a blender 1/3 at a time and blend until smooth. Lastly, add salt, Tabasco sauce, and cucumber. Chill. Serve chilled using a small amount of finely chopped green onion as a garnish.

MIXED GREEN VEGETABLES WITH SAUCE

1 1/2 cups Kraft mayonnaise   dash Tabasco sauce
3 hard boiled eggs, minced   1 medium onion, grated
4 tablespoons Wesson oil or   1 cup frozen cut green beans, cooked
   Crisco oil   1 cup frozen green peas, cooked
1 tablespoon Worcestershire   1 cup frozen baby green limas,
   sauce   cooked

Mix sauce ingredients well. Serve at room temperature on top of a combination of cooked peas, limas, and green beans. Sauce will keep a long time refrigerated.

5

Breads

BANANA BREAD

1/2 cup butter
1 cup sugar
3 eggs
3 ripe bananas, mashed
2 cups flour
1/2 teaspoon baking powder
1/2 teaspoon baking soda
1/2 teaspoon salt
1/2 cup pecans, chopped

In electric mixer cream butter and sugar. Add eggs and mix well. Add bananas. Sift flour, baking powder, baking soda, and salt. Add in dry ingredients 1/4 cup at a time, mixing well after each addition. Stir in pecans. Pour batter into a well-greased loaf pan and bake at 350 degrees for 1 hour or until an inserted toothpick comes out clean.

PECAN ROLLS

  1 yeast cake or 1 envelope yeast
  2 teaspoons lukewarm water
1/2 cup milk
  2 tablespoons butter
1/4 cup sugar
1/2 teaspoon salt
  1 egg, beaten
2 1/2 cups flour plus flour for kneading
  1 stick of butter (approximate)
1/2 cup brown sugar, plus brown sugar for muffin tins
    pecan halves

Soften yeast in lukewarm water. Scald milk in top of double boiler and add butter. Remove from heat and allow to cool to lukewarm. Combine all in large bowl and add sugar, salt, and yeast. Add 1 cup of flour and well-beaten egg and mix well by hand. Add 1 1/2 cups flour to make a stiff dough that can be kneaded.

Turn onto a lightly floured board and knead until dough is smooth and elastic. Put dough into a lightly greased (oiled) bowl and cover with a clean dry towel. Place in warm spot out of drafts and allow dough to rise until double in size.

Turn dough onto a floured board, knead, then roll dough into an oblong sheet about 1/4 inch thick. Brush dough with melted butter and sprinkle with brown sugar. Roll dough up like a jelly roll about 2 inches in diameter. Cut into 1 inch lengths. Grease muffin tins, put in bottom a dot of butter, 1 scant teaspoon of brown sugar, and 2 or 3 pecan halves. Put 1 stick of rolled dough in each cup. Cover with a clean dry towel and allow to rise until double in size. Bake in preheated 425 degree oven for about 20 minutes. Repeat.

YEAST ROLLS

This recipe belongs to Luvada Maney, who made these rolls for Mother. Lu came from Murfreesboro to be my baby nurse in 1935!

- 1/2 stick oleo
- 1 cup milk
- 1 teaspoon salt
- 1/4 cup sugar
- 1 yeast cake or package
- 2 tablespoons lukewarm water
- 1 egg, beaten
- 3 1/2–4 cups flour

Melt butter or oleo. Add milk. Add to sugar and salt. Dissolve yeast in lukewarm water. Combine all and add egg, flour, and yeast to make a soft dough. Let it rise once. Punch dough down to remove air. Roll out on a floured pastry board or cloth to about 1/2 inch thickness. Cut dough in circles with a biscuit cutter. Fold each circle of dough in half.

These may be frozen for 4 to 5 days. If frozen, remove from freezer, place on a baking sheet. Brush the tops of the rolls with melted butter. Let the rolls thaw and rise for about 2 hours (until double in size). Bake in a preheated 425 degree oven for 15 minutes.

CORN STICKS

1   cup plain corn meal
1   cup milk
1/4   teaspoon baking soda
1/4   teaspoon salt
1   egg
1   teaspoon Crisco or lard, melted

Beat egg, then add milk. Sift baking soda, salt, and corn meal together. Add to egg and milk. Add melted Crisco or lard. Grease tins and have them hot. Bake in preheated 425 degree oven for 20 minutes or until golden brown.

SKILLET EGG BREAD

1   egg
2   cups plain corn meal
1 1/2   cups buttermilk
1   teaspoon baking soda
1   teaspoon baking powder
1   teaspoon salt

Mix slightly beaten egg with buttermilk. Sift together plain corn meal, baking soda, baking powder, and salt. Add and mix all ingredients well. Preheat a heavy skillet well seasoned with oil until very warm. Place on low heat on top of stove. Pour in batter. When the bottom and sides are browned and the center is almost set and bubbly, the cake should be set enough to turn. Turn the cake of bread over and brown that side. Serve hot.

STONEWALL JACKSON SPOON BREAD

3 eggs, beaten
1 cup plain corn meal
1 teaspoon sugar
1 teaspoon salt
1 heaping teaspoon baking powder
3 cups milk
2 tablespoons butter

Mix eggs, corn meal, sugar, salt, and baking powder. Add milk gradually. Melt butter in a 2 quart casserole or 6 1/2 x 10 inch glass baking dish. Pour batter over it. Bake in 425 degree preheated oven for 20 minutes. Reduce heat to 325 degrees and continue cooking for an additional 30 to 40 minutes. If cooking in a metal pan, increase temperature about 25 degrees.

CORN BREAD

2 cups plain corn meal
1/4 teaspoon salt
1/2 teaspoon baking soda
2 tablespoons Crisco, melted
1 cup buttermilk

Sift together the dry ingredients. Mix with melted shortening and buttermilk. Put in a hot, well-greased 10 inch cast iron skillet. This recipe can be cooked in an 8 or 9 inch square or 6 x 10 inch rectangular baking pan. Bake in a preheated 425 degree oven for 20 to 25 minutes. Adjust cooking time as needed.

NUT BREAD

   1 egg, slightly beaten
   1 cup sugar
   1 cup milk
2 1/2 cups flour
  1/2 cup pecans, chopped
   2 teaspoons baking powder
  1/2 teaspoon salt

Mix all ingredients together. Pour the batter into a well-greased loaf pan and bake at 350 degrees about 45 minutes.

CHEESE BISCUITS

   2 cups flour
   4 teaspoons baking powder
  1/2 teaspoon salt
  1/2 cup sharp cheddar cheese, grated
   4 tablespoons solid shortening (Crisco)
  3/4 cup milk

Sift together flour, baking powder, and salt. Add grated cheese and mix well. Add Crisco and cut in with pastry knife until mixture has the look and consistency of coarse meal. Moisten to a soft dough using milk. Turn soft dough out on a lightly floured pastry board or cloth. Dust with flour and roll out to about 3/4 inch thick. Cut with a floured biscuit cutter. Bake in preheated 450 degree oven for 12 to 14 minutes.

CHRISTMAS BREAD

1/2 cup sugar
1 egg
1 1/4 cups milk

3 cups Bisquick
1 cup pecans, chopped
1 cup mixed (candied) fruit

Mix 1 cup of Bisquick with fruit and nuts. Slightly beat egg and add sugar, milk, and 2 cups of Bisquick. Mix well and add the Bisquick, fruit, and nuts, stirring to mix. Turn into a well-greased loaf pan. Bake in preheated 350 degree oven for 45 to 50 minutes. Cool on rack.

CRANBERRY BREAD

1 cup sugar
1 egg
2 cups flour
1/2 teaspoon salt
1/2 teaspoon baking powder
1/2 teaspoon baking soda

2 tablespoons butter, melted
2 tablespoons hot water
1/2 cup orange juice
3/4 cup fresh cranberries,
    cut in half
1/2 cup pecans, chopped

Beat egg in large mixer bowl. Add sugar. Sift all dry ingredients together. Add dry ingredients, melted butter, hot water, and orange juice. Mix well and fold in cranberries and pecans. Turn batter into a well-greased, floured loaf pan and bake in a preheated 325 degree oven for about 1 hour and 10 minutes. Turn out and cool on a rack.

WAFFLES

1 cup flour
3 teaspoons baking powder
1/2 teaspoon salt
1 tablespoon sugar

2 eggs, separated
1 cup milk
3 tablespoons butter

Sift dry ingredients together. Beat egg yolks well. Add milk. Add dry ingredients. Melt butter and add. Beaten egg whites should be folded into batter last. Pour into a hot waffle iron.

Granddaughter Lyssa with white cake decorated with white icing.

48

6

Cakes

WHITE CAKE

Cakes were Mother's best! She always used Parkay oleo and square 9 inch pans! No round!

      3/4 cup oleo (1 1/2 sticks)
   1 3/4 cups sugar, plus 2 tablespoons
         1 cup milk, plus 2 tablespoons
         3 cups Swansdown cake flour, sifted
      3/4 teaspoon salt
         4 teaspoons baking powder
         1 teaspoon vanilla
         5 egg whites

Cream oleo and sugar. Add vanilla. Add dry ingredients that have been sifted together 3 times alternating with milk. Fold in beaten egg whites. Grease with oleo the sides of two 9 inch cake pans and line the bottoms with waxed paper. Bake at 375 degrees for 25 to 30 minutes (until the cake springs back when lightly touched with a finger).

Mother serving her wedding cake at granddaughter Lyssa's wedding.

COCONUT CAKE

Make white cake and white icing (see recipe on p. 63). Put some coconut on top of icing between layers and then cover entire cake after icing with coconut. Use fresh or frozen coconut—not canned!

ANGEL FOOD CAKE

- 1 cup plus 2 tablespoons flour
- 1/2 cup sugar
- 1 cup sugar
- 1 teaspoon vanilla
- 1 1/2 cups egg whites
- 1/4 teaspoon salt
- 1 1/2 teaspoons cream of tartar

Sift together the flour and 1/2 cup sugar five times. Sift separately 1 cup sugar. Beat egg whites and salt until they stand in peaks, but are not dry. When foamy, add cream of tartar. Slowly add sugar. Add vanilla. Fold in flour and sugar mixture. Pour into an angel food cake pan. Rap pan on table several times and cut batter with a knife before baking. Bake at 350 degrees about 30 to 40 minutes. To cool, invert cake pan over bottle neck. This will ensure desired height.

COCONUT SNOWBALLS

Ice angel food cake squares with white icing. Roll in either fresh or frozen coconut. Not canned!

RUM CAKES

Mix together 2 boxes powdered sugar and 1 stick melted butter. Thin with a little milk and rum extract. Dip angel food cake squares in mixture and roll them in finely chopped pecans.

51

CHOCOLATE ANGEL FOOD CAKE

My favorite and the one I always wanted for my birthday iced with peppermint icing!!

1 cup flour	1 2/3 cups egg whites
1/4 cup cocoa	1/4 teaspoon salt
1/2 cup sugar	1 1/2 teaspoons cream of tartar
1 cup sugar	

Sift together flour, cocoa, and 1/2 cup sugar five times. Sift separately 1 cup sugar. Beat the egg whites and salt until they stand in peaks but are not dry. When foamy, add cream of tartar. Slowly add sugar. Fold in flour mixture. Pour into an angel food cake pan. Rap pan on table and cut batter with a knife before baking. Bake at 350 degrees for about 40 to 45 minutes. To cool, invert cake pan over bottle neck to ensure desired height.

YELLOW ANGEL FOOD CAKE

1 cup egg yolks	1/2 teaspoon cream of tartar
pinch of salt	1/2 teaspoon baking powder
1/2 cup water	1/2 teaspoon lemon extract
1 cup sugar	1/2 teaspoon vanilla extract
1 1/2 cups Swansdown cake flour	

Beat egg yolks, salt, and water 15 minutes at high speed on the mixer. Fold in sugar. Sift dry ingredients 5 times and fold in. Add flavorings. Bake at 350 degrees about 50 minutes in an angel food cake pan. To cool, invert cake pan over bottle neck to ensure desired height.

DAFFODIL CAKE

This recipe came from Leah Robson of Wilmette, Illinois, who is a wonderful cook. The Robsons were very old and dear friends of my parents and our families visited together a lot. My father grew up with Leah in Chicago.

6 eggs	1/2 teaspoon almond extract
pinch of salt	2 teaspoons cold water
1/2 teaspoon cream of tartar	1/2 teaspoon vanilla
3/4 cup sugar	1/2 teaspoon baking powder
1 cup cake flour	

Separate eggs. Beat egg whites until foamy. Add cream of tartar and beat until stiff. Beat in 1/2 cup sugar. Sift 1/2 cup flour and 1/4 cup sugar 4 times. Fold together all ingredients. Add almond extract. In separate bowl, beat egg yolks well and slowly add 1/2 cup sugar. Continue to beat and add cold water, vanilla, and 1/2 cup cake flour sifted 3 times with baking powder. Pour white mixture into angel food cake pan. Pour yellow mixture on top. Run a knife through batter. Bake at 350 degrees for 30 minutes and then at 275 degrees for 30 minutes. Invert to cool before removing.

DEVIL'S FOOD CAKE

2/3 cup oleo	1/4 teaspoon salt
1 1/2 cups sugar	1 teaspoon vanilla
2 1/2 cups sifted Swansdown cake flour	3 eggs, separated
1 teaspoon baking powder	1 cup buttermilk
1 teaspoon baking soda	3 squares Baker's unsweetened chocolate, melted

Cream sugar and oleo together. Add egg yolks one at a time. Add dry ingredients alternating with milk. Add chocolate. Beat egg whites and fold in. Grease with oleo the sides of two 9 inch cake pans and line the bottoms with waxed paper. Bake at 350 degrees for 25 to 30 minutes. Check for doneness.

DARK FRUIT CAKE

3/4 pound butter
3 cups sugar
2 1/2 cups flour
7 eggs
1 teaspoon cloves, ground
1 teaspoon cinnamon, ground
1 teaspoon nutmeg, ground
1 teaspoon allspice, ground
1/2 pound dates, chopped
2 pounds raisins
1 pound currants

3/4 pound pecans
1/2 pound figs, chopped
3/4 pound almonds
1/2 pound citron
1 pound cut cherries
1/2 pound cut pineapple, candied
1/4 pound orange peel, candied
1/4 pound lemon peel, candied
1 teaspoon baking powder
whiskey
cheesecloth

Soak fruit overnight in whiskey. Cream butter and sugar. Add eggs and flour. Fold in nuts and fruits. Pour into a greased, paper-lined tube or bread pans. Bake 250 degrees about 5 to 6 hours. Cool before removing from pan. When cake has cooled, soak 2 yards of 100 percent cotton cheesecloth in whiskey and wrap cake. Then wrap and seal into heavy duty foil and refrigerate. If kept more than 6 weeks prior to serving, rewet cheesecloth in whiskey every 3 to 4 weeks.

LIGHT FRUIT CAKE

12 eggs
1 pound butter
2 pounds sugar
1/2 teaspoon baking powder
2 1/2 pounds flour
1 pound almonds
1 pound pecans

1 pound citron
2 pounds pineapple, candied
2 pounds cherries, candied
2 pounds figs
1/2 tablespoon powdered mace
3 cans southern dried coconut
15–20 drops of oil of cinnamon

Chop nuts and fruits and dredge with 1/2 cup of flour. Cream butter and sugar. Add well-beaten eggs and flour. Fold in nuts and fruits. Pour into greased, paper-lined tube pans or bread pans. Bake at 250 degrees about 5 to 6 hours. Soak in whiskey. (See notes on dark fruit cake.) Decorate top of cake with some pecan halves.

HICKORY NUT CAKE

3/4 cup oleo or butter
2 cups sifted sugar
4 eggs
1/2 cup milk

3 1/2 cups sifted Swansdown cake flour
2 teaspoons baking powder
1 cup hickory nuts
1/2 teaspoon vanilla

Separate eggs. Beat yolks separately until lemony; whites until stiff but not dry. Mix as for any butter cake. Coat hickory nuts with 1/4 cup of the sifted flour before adding. Fold egg whites into batter last. Bake at 350 degrees in two 9 inch greased and lined pans, for 30 to 40 minutes (until tested done).

If desired, ice with caramel icing (see recipe on p. 61) to which another cup of hickory nuts have been added.

JAM CAKE

1 cup sugar
1 cup blackberry jam
2 1/2 cups Swansdown cake flour
3/4 teaspoon baking powder
1/2 cup buttermilk
3 eggs, separated

1 teaspoon baking soda
3/4 cup oleo or butter
1 teaspoon nutmeg
1 teaspoon cinnamon
1/2 teaspoon allspice
1 cup pecans, chopped

Cream oleo and sugar. Add egg yolks. Sift spices with cake flour 3 times. Alternate adding dry ingredients with buttermilk. Beat egg whites and fold into batter. Mix in blackberry jam. Bake in two 9 inch greased and lined cake pans. Bake at 350 degrees for 30 to 35 minutes. Ice with caramel icing (see recipe on p. 61) to which chopped pecans have been added.

PRUNE CAKE

No one would order Mother's prune cake until she renamed it Tahitian cake. When it became popular, she called it prune cake again.

    1/2 cup oleo
  1 1/4 cups sugar
      3 eggs, separated
  2 1/2 cups Swansdown cake flour
      3 teaspoons baking powder
      1 teaspoon nutmeg
      1 teaspoon cinnamon
      1 cup prunes, cooked and chopped
      1 cup milk

Cream oleo and sugar. Add egg yolks. Sift spices with cake flour and add. Add prunes and milk. Beat egg whites until stiff but not dry and fold into batter. Bake in two 9 inch cake pans in which the sides have been greased and the bottoms lined with waxed paper. Bake at 350 degrees for 30 to 35 minutes. Spread with filling (see below).

FILLING FOR PRUNE CAKE

    1/2 cup prunes
    1/4 cup raisins
    1/4 cup dates, chopped
    1/3 cup sugar
      2 egg yolks
    1/2 cup milk

Cook all ingredients until thick. Remove and add 1 tablespoon butter, 1 teaspoon of vanilla, and 1/2 cup chopped pecans.

Spread between layers of cakes. Ice with white icing.

CARAMEL FUDGE CAKE

4 tablespoons butter
1 cup brown sugar
1 egg
1 cup flour
1 cup pecans, chopped
1 teaspoon baking powder
1 teaspoon vanilla
  pinch of salt

Cream butter and brown sugar. Stir in remaining ingredients. Bake in a well-greased, 9 inch, square pan at 350 degrees 25 to 30 minutes. Cool, cut into squares and roll in powdered sugar.

CHOCOLATE FUDGE CAKE

2 squares Baker's chocolate
1 stick butter
2 eggs
1 cup sugar

1 teaspoon salt
1 teaspoon vanilla
1/2 cup flour
1 cup pecans, chopped

Melt together chocolate squares and butter. Set aside. Beat eggs and add remaining ingredients. Add chocolate and butter mixture. Put batter in a well-greased 9 inch square pan. Bake at 350 degrees about 25 to 30 minutes Cool. Ice with fudge cake icing (see recipe on p. 62). Cut into squares.

7

Cookies

CRESCENTS

1/2 pound butter
8 tablespoons powdered sugar

2 1/2 cups flour
2 teaspoons lemon extract

Cream butter and sugar. Add flavoring, then flour. Makes a stiff dough. Add some chopped pecans, if desired, and shape into crescents or balls. Bake on parchment on a cookie sheet in a moderate oven, 300 to 325 degrees, until bottoms of cookies start to brown, approximately 20 minutes.

CHOCOLATE COOKIES

1 heaping cup brown sugar
1/2 cup butter
1 egg
1/2 cup sour milk
1/2 teaspoon baking soda

2 1/4 cups flour
2 squares chocolate, melted
1 teaspoon vanilla
1 cup pecans, chopped

Sour milk can be buttermilk or milk with a few drops of vinegar or lemon juice. Dissolve baking soda in a little water. Mix all ingredients well. Drop dough by spoonfuls onto a cookie sheet and bake in a 350 degree oven for 12 to 17 minutes. Ice with uncooked chocolate icing (see recipe on p. 62).

CHEESE DATE COOKIES

1/2 pound cheddar cheese
1/4 pound butter
  2 cups flour
1/4 teaspoon salt
  2 8 ounce boxes dates
1/4 pound pecans

Finely grate the cheese. Allow butter and cheese to reach a softened room temperature. Mix well with flour and salt to make a stiff paste. Stuff dates with the pecans. Wrap cookie-sized pieces of dough around a pecan-stuffed date. Lay cookies seam side down on cookie sheet and bake at 400 degrees for 12 to 15 minutes. Cool before removing from pan.

ICEBOX COOKIES

1/2 pound butter
1/2 cup sugar
  1 teaspoon cinnamon
1/4 teaspoon allspice
1/4 teaspoon cloves
1/3 cup molasses
2 1/2 cups sifted flour
3/4 cup pecans, chopped

Mix all ingredients. Make into a roll and refrigerate overnight. Slice dough thin and place cookies on a baking sheet one inch apart. Bake in preheated 325 degree oven for 12 to 15 minutes or until the edges are very lightly brown. Do not overcook—they burn quickly.

CHINESE CHEWS

    1 cup chopped dates
    1 cup chopped pecans
    1 cup powdered sugar
  3/4 cup flour
    2 eggs, beaten
    1 teaspoon baking powder
       pinch salt

Mix sugar and flour. Add eggs, nuts, and dates. Spread batter in a well-buttered 9 inch square cake pan. Bake in a preheated 350 degree oven for 20 to 30 minutes, until a toothpick comes out clean. Cool, cut in squares, and roll in granulated sugar.

SOUR CREAM MUFFINS

This is one of my favorites! The first house I lived in was on Brightwood Avenue. This recipe came from our neighbors, the Wards.

    1 cup sour cream
1 1/2 cups flour
    1 cup sugar
    1 egg
  1/4 teaspoon baking powder
  1/2 teaspoon cinnamon
2 1/2 teaspoons allspice
    1 teaspoon baking soda
  1/2 teaspoon cloves
       pecans (optional)

Cream sugar and egg. Add dry ingredients. Add sour cream last to which baking soda has been added. Pecans can be added. Bake at 375 degrees in paper lined muffin tins for about 20 minutes or until an inserted toothpick comes out clean.

8

Icing and Candy

CARAMEL ICING

- 4 cups white granulated sugar
- 2 tablespoons plus 2 teaspoons flour
  pinch salt (1/8 teaspoon or less)
- 1 1/3 cups whole milk
- 1 1/2 sticks butter
- 1 teaspoon vanilla

Put 3/4 cup sugar into a very heavy skillet over a very low heat. Heat, stirring constantly with a long handled metal spoon for 8 to 10 minutes until the sugar is melted and is a light golden tan color. Remove the pan from the heat.

In a pot, add flour and a pinch of salt to the remaining 3 1/4 cups of sugar. Stir the milk in until smooth. Bring to a boil, stirring constantly. Very carefully and slowly add the melted browned sugar and cook to 400 degrees on a candy thermometer. Remove from heat and place the pot in a pan of tap water to cool down to 110 degrees. Add butter and vanilla. Beat with electric hand mixer until creamy and spreadable.

Grandson Bobby with white cake with chocolate icing.

CHOCOLATE ICING

3 cups sugar	1 1/2 sticks butter
3/4 cup cocoa	1/4 teaspoon salt
3/4 cup milk	

Combine all ingredients and cook to soft ball stage. Set in a pan of water to cool down. Beat with mixer until spreadable.

CHOCOLATE ICING FOR FUDGE CAKE

1 cup sugar	1/4 cup butter
1/4 cup cocoa	1/2 cup milk

Combine all ingredients and cook to soft ball stage. Set in a pan of water and cool down to 110 degrees. Beat with mixer until creamy and spreadable.

UNCOOKED ICING FOR CHOCOLATE COOKIES

1 box powdered sugar
5 tablespoons cocoa
4 tablespoons melted butter

Mix ingredients in medium bowl. Thin with milk until spreadable or add 1/2 cup coffee if desired.

WHITE ICING

4 egg whites
2 1/2 cups sugar
1 tablespoon light Karo syrup
    pinch of cream of tartar
1/2 cup water
1 teaspoon vanilla

Combine all ingredients except egg whites and cook to soft ball stage. Slowly add to beaten egg whites. Continue beating with mixer. Add 1 teaspoon vanilla.

PEPPERMINT ICING

Make white icing (above) omitting vanilla and adding peppermint extract to taste. Tint with red food color.

DIVINITY

2 1/2 cups sugar
  1/3 cup water
  2/3 cup light Karo syrup

2 egg whites
1/2 teaspoon vanilla

Combine all ingredients except egg whites and cook to soft ball stage. Pour over beaten egg whites. Add vanilla. Beat until mixture can be dropped by the spoonful onto waxed paper. Cool.

PRALINES

  1/3 cup white sugar, browned
2 2/3 cups white sugar
    1 box light brown sugar
  1/2 pint half and half

1/4 pint milk
3/4 cup light Karo syrup
  1 pound pecans,
       coarsely chopped

Stir all ingredients (except 1/3 cup white sugar, browned) well. Cook over low heat, stirring constantly until sugar is dissolved. Add 1/3 cup sugar, browned in the same method as used in caramel icing (see recipe on p. 61). Drop by the spoonful onto waxed paper or a buttered cookie sheet and let sit long enough to cool completely and set. Put into an airtight container.

CANDY (SIMILAR TO PRALINES)

1 box brown sugar
2 cups white sugar
2 tablespoons light Karo syrup
1 cup cream

1/4 cup milk
  2 teaspoons vanilla
1/2 stick butter

Combine brown sugar, white sugar, Karo syrup, cream, and milk. Cook slowly to soft ball stage. Add vanilla and butter, melted and browned. Cool over water. Do not beat. Drop by spoonful on a buttered platter.

9

Pies and Desserts

PASTRY

Except for her peach pie, Mother always made pies in individual pastry shells.

  1 cup Crisco
1/2 cup water
1 1/2 cups sifted flour
1/2 teaspoon salt
  1 teaspoon baking powder

Melt Crisco and water. Add flour, salt, and baking powder. Mix well, cover and refrigerate. When dough is chilled through, turn onto a floured pastry board or cloth. Gently roll with rolling pin in all directions, being careful not to stretch the dough. Place a large circle of dough over pie pan or individual pie tins. Gently fit it to the contours of the pan. Trim the edges and flute with fingers or fork for decoration. Crust is ready to be filled with fillings that are to be cooked in pastry.

For pies using a pre-baked crust, prick the bottom of pie shell generously with a fork and bake in preheated oven at 450 degrees for 10 to 12 minutes or until golden brown.

FRIED PIES

Use pie pastry recipe on page 65 and roll thin. Cut with round cutter 3 inches to 6 inches in diameter. (Small 3-inch size would be for a party). Spread with cooked fruit mixture of your choice on one half. Fold over and crimp edges together with a fork. Either fry or bake at 425 degrees until brown. After cooling, sprinkle with powdered sugar.

Cooked peaches or apples will not take as much sugar to sweeten as cooked apricots. Sugar to taste.

CHESS PIES

1 stick butter or oleo
2 cups sugar
2 tablespoons flour
2 tablespoons corn meal
1 teaspoon vanilla
5 egg yolks
1 cup milk

Cream butter and sugar. Add remaining ingredients. Put into unbaked individual pastry shells (see recipe on p. 65). Sprinkle pies with nutmeg. Bake 15 minutes at 425 degrees. Reduce to 375 degrees and continue baking until pies don't shake. (Makes 12–14 small pies.)

MERINGUE PIE TOPPING

2 egg whites
1 heaping tablespoon sugar
1/4 teaspoon vanilla

Beat egg whites until stiff. Add sugar gradually. Add vanilla. Spread on pie and brown in preheated 350 degree oven for 10 to 15 minutes.

CHOCOLATE PIES

3 squares chocolate	1/2 teaspoon salt
2 1/2 cups cold milk	4 egg yolks, beaten
4 tablespoons flour	2 tablespoons butter
1 cup sugar	2 teaspoons vanilla

Scald the milk with the chocolate. Beat until mixture is smooth. Combine flour, sugar, and salt. Add to egg yolks. Pour a small amount of chocolate mixture a little at a time over yolks and flour mixture, stirring vigorously. Cook until thickened in a double boiler. Add butter and vanilla. Cool and put in baked pastry shells (see recipe on p. 65). Top with meringue or whipped cream.

COCONUT CREAM PIES

This was in the Murfreesboro Cook Book, dated 1914.

2 eggs, separated	1/2 cup milk
1 cup sugar	1 teaspoon flour
1/2 coconut, grated	

In a double boiler, cook egg yolks, sugar, grated coconut, milk, and flour. Beat all together and stir constantly while cooking until thickened. Put in pastry lined pans (see recipe on p. 65). Use whites for meringue (see recipe on p. 66).

CHOCOLATE FUDGE PIES

1 stick butter	1/4 cup flour
2 squares Baker's chocolate	1 teaspoon salt
1 cup sugar	1 teaspoon vanilla
2 eggs	

Melt chocolate, take off fire, and stir in sugar. Add 2 whole eggs beaten slightly. Add flour, salt, and vanilla. Pour in greased pie pan or pans and bake 400 degrees about 25 minutes. Serve with whipped cream or ice cream (vanilla or peppermint are good).

LEMON PIES

1 1/2 cups sugar
  2 cups boiling water
  5 tablespoons cornstarch
  5 tablespoons flour

4 egg yolks
4 tablespoons lemon rind, grated
6 tablespoons lemon juice
2 teaspoons butter

Mix cornstarch, flour, and sugar. Add boiling water very slowly stirring rapidly and constantly. Add butter, lemon rind, and lemon juice. Slowly add beaten egg yolks stirring rapidly and constantly. Pour into prebaked pastry shell or shells (see recipe on p.65), top with meringue, and brown. Chill to serve.

PECAN PIES

3 eggs
1 cup white sugar
1 cup dark Karo syrup

1 cup pecans, chopped
1 tablespoon butter
1 teaspoon vanilla

Mix all ingredients. Put in individual pastry shells (see recipe on p. 65). Place pecan halves on top (in design if desired) before baking. Bake at 425 degrees for 10 minutes. Reduce to 350 degrees and continue to bake for 40 to 45 minutes or until pies set.

PEACH PIE

6 peaches
1 cup sugar
1 tablespoon flour

1 tablespoon butter, melted
1 egg

Bake pie crust (see recipe on p. 65) for 8 minutes. Cream sugar, flour, and melted butter. Beat egg well and add. Pour mixture over peaches in baked shell. Bake in a slow oven at 275 degrees for several hours. A crustiness forms over the top when done.

CARAMEL DESSERT SAUCE

2 cups brown sugar
2 tablespoons flour
1 cup milk
2 tablespoons butter
  pinch of salt
1 teaspoon vanilla

Cook all ingredients until dissolved and boil about 2 minutes. Add butter, salt, and vanilla.

CHOCOLATE DESSERT SAUCE

6 squares unsweetened chocolate, melted
2 cups sugar
1 12 ounce can evaporated milk
1 1/2 teaspoons vanilla
2 tablespoons butter
  pinch of salt

Melt chocolate over hot water. Add sugar gradually. When blended, add evaporated milk, vanilla, salt, butter. Cook no longer than to blend well. Refrigerate.

CHOCOLATE SOUFFLE

2 tablespoons butter
1 1/2 tablespoons flour
3/4 cup milk
1 1/2 squares Baker's chocolate
1 cup sugar
3 eggs, separated
1/2 teaspoon vanilla

Melt chocolate squares. Melt butter, add flour, and stir until smooth. Add milk stirring constantly. When mixture boils, add melted chocolate, then sugar. Add this mixture to beaten egg yolks. Cool slightly and fold in stiffly beaten egg whites. Add vanilla. Put in straight sided, ungreased souffle dish. Place dish in a pan of boiling water and bake for 20 minutes in 350 degree oven. Serve immediately with whipped cream or peppermint ice cream.

ORANGE CHARLOTTE RUSSE

1 envelope Knox gelatin
1/4 cup hot water
1/4 cup cold water
1 cup orange juice
1 cup sugar
3 egg yolks
1 pint whipped cream

Soak gelatin in cold water. Dissolve in hot water. Mix orange juice and sugar well. Beat egg yolks well and add to juice mixture. Add gelatin and refrigerate. When it begins to thicken, add whipped cream. Pour into a mold lined with lady fingers. May be garnished with whipped cream, coconut, or mandarin orange sections.

MERINGUES

These can be used like pastry shells or shaped into cookies.

    1 cup egg whites
2 1/4 cups sugar
    1 teaspoon vanilla

Beat egg whites until stiff. Slowly add 1 1/2 cups sugar. Beating constantly, add vanilla and 3/4 cup sugar. Drop by the spoonful about 3 inches apart on a waxed paper-lined cookie sheet. Shape so ice cream can be scooped into center. Put in a preheated 300 degree oven. Reduce to 250 degrees and bake for about 1 hour. Do NOT brown.

Nuts and dates can be added if made smaller to resemble cookies.

AMBROSIA

A favorite southern dish whether used as a fruit salad with the meal or with fruit cake when the desserts are served.

    1 dozen oranges   1 pound grated coconut
    1 can crushed pineapple   1–2 cups sugar

Make the day before serving.

Using a sharp knife, peel the oranges removing all the outside white membrane from the sections. Cut out pulp from between connective membrane. Remove seeds. Use fresh grated or frozen coconut. Mix in a large bowl. Cover tightly and refrigerate until time to serve.

ENGLISH TOFFEE DESSERT

    1   cup crushed vanilla wafers
    3   eggs, separated
    1   cup pecans, chopped
    1   cup powdered sugar
  1/4   pound butter
1 1/2   squares unsweetened Baker's chocolate, melted
  1/2   teaspoon vanilla

Mix vanilla wafer crumbs and nuts. Put half of the mixture on bottom of a 9 x 9 or 6 x 10 inch buttered pan. Cream butter and sugar. Add the egg yolks, chocolate, and vanilla. Add the beaten egg whites. Pour over crumbs and top with remaining crumbs. Chill.

CORNFLAKE RING

    1   cup brown sugar
1 1/2   tablespoons Karo syrup
  1/3   cup milk
    3   tablespoons butter
    4   cups cornflakes

Cook Karo, milk, butter, and sugar to a soft ball stage. Pour into a large buttered bowl. Add cornflakes. Mix well. Pack into a well-buttered mold and let stand until cool. **Do not chill.** Unmold and serve with coffee ice cream in the center.

RICE PUDDING

2 eggs
2 cups milk
1/4 teaspoon salt
1/2 cup sugar
1 1/3 cups cooked rice
       dash cinnamon
1 teaspoon vanilla

Beat eggs well. Add milk, salt, sugar, cinnamon, and vanilla. Stir in rice. Pour pudding mix into a 1 or 1 1/2 quart casserole dish. Set dish into a pan of boiling water 1/2 the depth of the casserole dish. Bake at about 350 degrees for about 30 minutes until pudding is set.

BREAD PUDDING

1 cup bread crumbs, packed tightly
2 cups milk
2 eggs, separated
1/2 cup sugar
2 tablespoons butter, melted
1 lemon

Beat egg yolks. Grate lemon rind, reserving juice. Melt butter. Combine all with bread crumbs, milk, and sugar. Put into a 1 or 1 1/2 quart casserole dish. Set the dish into a pan of boiling water 1/2 the depth of the casserole dish. Bake at 350 degrees until pudding thickens, about 1/2 an hour. Remove and squeeze juice of the lemon over pudding. Cover with meringue (see recipe on p. 66) and put back into the oven for 8 to 10 minutes to brown.

73

MARSHMALLOW PUDDING

I have never had this but have heard Mother talk about it as the recipe came from Mrs. A. L. Todd from Murfreesboro.

Dissolve 1 heaping tablespoon of Knox gelatin in 1 pint cold water. Dissolve by heating, stirring constantly. Pour this slowly over the whites of 6 eggs beaten stiff and keep beating. Pour 1 pint sugar over the whites in the same manner. Add 1 teaspoon almond extract. Divide into 3 parts. Color 1 part pink. Put 1 part of white mixture in a lightly oiled glass pie pan, sprinkle with chopped pecans. Put in the pink layer, then another layer of pecans and then another layer of white. Let cool. Slice and serve with whipped cream.

MARSHMALLOW DATE ROLL

Recipe 1 was written when Mother measured bought ingredients by how much they cost and of course she knew exactly what she meant. Recipe 2 is a modern adaptation.

Recipe 1
Cut up 1 10-cent box marshmallows and soak 15 minutes in 1/2 cup milk. Add 15-cent package of cut dates (8 ounces) and 1 cup chopped pecans. Add 10-cent box graham crackers, crushed fine. Mix all well and roll into 1/2 cup crushed graham crackers. Refrigerate overnight.

Recipe 2
1 1/2 cups marshmallow cream
1 1/2 cups graham cracker crumbs
    1 8 ounce package of chopped dates
    1 cup chopped pecans

Mix ingredients together well and make into a roll. Roll the "roll" in 1/2 cup additional graham cracker crumbs. Refrigerate overnight and slice.

10

Beverages

BOILED CUSTARD

6 eggs, separated
1 cup sugar

2 tablespoons flour
1 quart milk

Beat egg yolks. Add remaining ingredients. Cook in a double boiler until thickened, stirring constantly. May be flavored individually with vanilla or bourbon.

EGG NOG

12 eggs, separated
1 cup sugar
1 cup bourbon
1 quart whipping cream

Beat egg yolks. Add sugar to egg whites and beat. Mix all together and add whipping cream. Must be made not too far ahead of serving and kept cold. To serve, top each cup with sweetened whipped cream and a dash of nutmeg.

FROZEN WHISKEY SOURS

1 small can frozen lemonade
2 cans bourbon
3 cans water
3 tablespoons orange juice

Mix together and freeze.

FROZEN DAIQUIRIS

1 small can frozen limeade
2 cans light rum
3 cans water

Mix well and freeze.

I hope you enjoy Mother's recipes as much as I have through the years.

Index